John Large

Mischiefs of the Malt Tax

John Large

Mischiefs of the Malt Tax

ISBN/EAN: 9783337425074

Printed in Europe, USA, Canada, Australia, Japan

Cover: Foto ©Suzi / pixelio.de

More available books at **www.hansebooks.com**

MISCHIEFS

OF THE

MALT TAX,

AND

REASONS FOR ITS TOTAL AND IMMEDIATE REPEAL,

AND

HOW IT MAY BE EFFECTED.

By **JOHN LARGE**, of Wootton Bassett,

Author of "SECRETS OF FARMING."

BATH :

PRINTED AT THE "CHRONICLE" OFFICE, KINGSTON BUILDINGS,

MDCCCLXIV.

PREFACE.

The object of this volume is to present to the public an outline of the manifold and serious evils attributable alone to the iniquitous Malt Tax. The author has endeavoured to explain how it affects and injures the Farmer, and how he (the agriculturist) may be placed in the same position as he was in the happy days of Protection; how this impost oppresses the poor man, and why it is he cannot attain to that which his Maker designed him to be, namely, a man of high moral principles and Christian feeling. Also, how its machinery affects every article of consumption, and how the income yielded by the tax may be replaced, so that the repeal shall not interfere with the necessary expenditure of the country. That the farmers of this kingdom have suffered most severely for many years no one can deny, and it is imperative that some change should be made in the legislation of

our country, to enable them to occupy the
same honourable position they formerly enjoyed. With regard to the labouring population, it is obvious that some arrangement
should be made to reform their degraded habit
of resorting to the alehouse, and to induce
them as much as possible to acquire a taste for
home comforts and blissful happiness, which
will incite them to study the works of their
Maker, and lead them to a determination of
preparing themselves for the world to come.
Some are continually complaining that the
poorer classes of the population are ill-cared
for, and above all, illiterate. The poor man
has no taste for reading in an alehouse.
Remove the tax, and then try him. Landed
proprietors will then build decent cottages,
farmers will be enabled to pay higher wages,
the poor man will be in a position to procure
a comfortable home and a barrel of beer to
keep him there! Then, and not till then, can
we hope to expect any permanent improve-
ment in the condition of the labouring population of this country.

MISCHIEFS

OF THE

MALT TAX.

————

Upon the Chancellor of the Exchequer devolves the duty of proposing taxes sufficient for the support and safety of our country. It is a sacred duty he has to perform; and I believe every subject of the realm, from the peer to the peasant, willingly submits, and cheerfully pays, with a ready heart and free hand, any and every tax excepting one. And which is that? Why, the "Malt Tax!" which is both unjust and unfair.

It may be questioned why unjust. Because the poor man is taxed higher than any other class; and how is it that we find he is taxed higher than any one else? Because the only beverage he can get, to support him from year to year through his daily toil (good wholesome beer) is taxed one penny per quart, one half-penny for every pint, and consequently one farthing for every time he opens his mouth to quench his parching thirst.

Now to solve this problem (for most assuredly a problem it is, the poor man not being sufficiently skilled in figures to ascertain the reason why, or how, it is he has to pay so much for the necessary support of his daily toil), I presume that one quarter of malt will make sixty-eight gallons of good, wholesome and strong ale; the tax on one quarter of malt is 22s. 8d., or 272 pence, which are the 68 gallons multiplied by 4—4d. per gallon tax, and 1d. per quart. I have already explained one penny per quart too much, I will now endeavour to find twopence more too much on the quart of the nation's natural beverage. If we can get rid of the malt tax, and abolish it altogether (it is no earthly use taking off half, or even two-thirds, for there will be the same expense in collecting), monopolizing brewers will have seen their day, malt will be manufactured in nearly (if not quite) every home, and where it is intended to be used; a quart of the best beer may then be produced for threepence per quart, instead of sixpence; and this will explain the other twopence.

The barley grower can also calculate to make 60s. per quarter of his crop more or less; I have already stated that one quarter of malt will make 68 gallons of good, strong ale or beer, and the quarter of barley will make the quarter of malt. We reckon the barley at 60s., and 8lbs. of hops at 1s. per lb. (for at that price they will be if the Malt Tax is repealed) will be 8s., making 68s., which is so far the cost of the 68 gallons of beer. Now, I consider there are ample means left (which may accrue from the second, and, moreover, a small quantity may reasonably be expected from a third quality from the same lot of malt) for defraying the various expenses incurred in malting, brewing, casks, &c.

We can then expect to have a good wholesome beverage free of any adulteration or narcotic drug at threepence per quart, with barley at 60s. per quarter. Oh ye landed proprietors and Members of Parliament! if you could but be convinced, would it not be instrumental in keeping up the price of land, and would you not one and all vote for the total abolition of the tax without further delay; for the day must come (with wheat at the present low price) when a reduction of from five to fifteen shillings per acre must take place on all arable land.

I should like to know what became of the 37,111,815 lbs. of tobacco last year. I have not said, nor do I intend to say, that brewers as a body use tobacco in the process of brewing; but this I do know, that 1lb. of tobacco will give as much additional strength to 68 gallons of beer as you can obtain from one bushel of good malt, and with malt at 9s. per bushel, it is a robbery of 5s. from the Exchequer. I have tried it myself, and can write from experience, and say that such is the case; it not only gives the additional strength, but it also causes an unnatural and premature ripeness, and, consequently, the beer will not keep for any length of time in a small cask. The brewer does not care for that, "we shall be happy to take to what is left," so he takes it home to the brewery, and it is then mixed again with other new beer.

Salt may also be used in brewing, which will necessarily increase the quantity, and diminish the Exchequer's receipts, and increase thirst. I do not apprehend that any serious consequences arise from the use of salt, beyond the creation of an unnatural thirst. With regard to the former named article, a multitude of evils must follow if tobacco is used in the process of brewing; it acts almost instantaneously as a stimulating narcotic, and excites the person to drink more than he requires, subsequently leading to intoxication, which is the foundation of all evil.

Teetotallers, perhaps, as a body, may not agree with me, but we may rest pretty well assured that if the adulteration of beer was unknown (and it is attributable alone to the tax), temperance meetings would never have sprung up; for every man would have enjoyed his wholesome beer by his own fireside, instead of going to the alehouse, where he has been probably tempted to take too much, tempted to do that which he ought not, and then, at last, he is tempted to resolve himself into the determination (if he is a sensible man) of joining the temperance society. We advocate temperance in all things, therefore have nothing to say against temperance meetings of any kind, but everyone must be cognizant of the fact that when persons drink nothing but water, they require, and will consume half as much again animal food as they would if they drank beer; thereby, again, showing the abomination of the Malt Tax; for it must necessarily increase the price of every kind of sort of meat, which everyone is complaining of.

Many persons willingly admit that there is a great deal of nourishment in wholesome, pure beer, but they say you are much stronger and better without it, provided you can get, and eat, as much animal food as you can. Now, such an one contradicts himself, for he admits there *is* much nutriment in beer, and yet it gives him no additional strength; they know they consume half as much again animal food, if they can get it, and having eaten as much as they can, they feel *so much* stronger, and that, for the present, they cannot obtain any more strength, unless they could devour more animal food. Now, if a man eats almost to repletion, he can always drink one pint of beer, and that must necessarily give him additional strength, according to their own admission.

Some persons will, probably, consider it ridiculous to suppose that barley will ever reach the high price of 60s. per quarter; I contend there is every possible chance, if the tax is abolished, of its making that price, unless there should be an extraordinary crop, when, as a matter of course, it would be lower, but I see no reason why good malting barley should not range from 50s. to 60s. per quarter, according to yield and quality. Wheat is at the price at which barley used to be formerly considered as a remunerating price to the grower; therefore, it is fair to allow barley to make the same price as wheat was supposed to make in former years, during the happy days of Protection, namely, 60s. per quarter, which was then considered to be a fair live and let live remunerating price.

If Protection is reversed into Free Trade, is it not fair and possible that the price of barley shall be reversed into the price of wheat? The British farmer may then expect, and hope, to be in the same comfortable position as he was in the days of Protection. As regards Protection to the farmer against foreign countries, we say it is gone, gone for ever; and as regards a fair free trade that will never appear, so long as the tax remains; therefore, it behoves all householders, rich and poor, young and old, landlords as well as tenants, to forward a petition, without delay, to the Chancellor of the Exchequer, praying for the total repeal of the Malt Tax, as being unfair, unjust, and abominably demoralizing in all its bearings.

A great proportion of the sin and crime of this nation may be attributed to this unfair tax. The field is so wide, and facilities are so great for adulteration, that few hesitate to avail themselves of the opportunity. That some narcotic drug is employed no reasonable man can deny, who has ever tasted public-house ale, and hence the origin of much crime and sin. From the effects of the narcotic drug, the poor man, as soon as he has drank the first half-pint, feels a sort of pleasurable excitement stealing over him ; it does not last for any length of time at first, but just long enough to tempt him to take more than is sufficient to do him good, and then it does not leave him until too late. He then goes on for a second, third, and fourth pint, and too frequently beyond that quantity ; the gallon of bread is swallowed in a few minutes, which would have brought a smile on many a crying and hungry child's face. Instead of being allowed to brew his own beer at home, he is continually brewing mischief and sin in all their hideous forms, when he is out. From excess over night, a nerveless affection of the mucous membrane of the stomach is the consequence on the following morning, which involves another pint or two to strengthen that organ ; but when it can be obtained, dram drinking is the recipe, and often followed up to a fearful extent.

Eventually poverty creeps into the poor man's dwelling, and what is to be done then ? His children are starving. Steal? No, he must not do that. He does not know what to do ; at last he makes up his mind to relate his troubles to an alehouse companion at the next meeting ; they then talk matters over, and at last agree to go on a poaching expedition. Prompted at first by destitution at home, they go boldly to work, thinking they will soon be able to obtain the necessaries of life which their starving families require. But, alas ! such is not the case. The money thus unjustly earned is almost invariably applied to the washing out of chalk marks at the alehouse, and in manufacturing a great many more ; and instead of mitigating the evil they complained of, they increase it to an un-limited extent. The drunkards then acquire courage to steal eggs, poultry, wood, sheep, corn from the field, as also the barn, and anything else they may happen to want; and murder is often committed to avoid detection.

Oh, ye honourable Peers and Members of the Commons House, are you aware that the unjust Malt Tax is the cause of all this? If so, pray abolish it altogether, without further delay. That such is the case, no one can deny. If the poor man could brew his own beer at home, he would not be tempted to *leave* home, and his attachment and fondness for his home and family would increase, in the same manner as his fondness for the alehouse did from the first time he entered it.

Now there are many who argue that if beer *was* cheaper the poor man would *then* resort to the alehouse for the sake of society. The argument does not apply, nor will it hold good, until the poor man has had an opportunity to seek that society in a more homely direction; namely, by being in a position with his barrel of beer at home to invite a friend or two (which he would do) and discourse on various topics, which will necessarily involve return visits, and a respectable occupation of their leisure evenings.

There are many evils connected with the alehouse. I consider the worst of all is, when a man is in the habit of going regularly every night; his poor wife at home anxiously waiting his return ; he comes home at last, and how does he come? Why, often ten thousand times worse than a brute beast; instead of bringing her home a mouthful of beer (of which he has taken too much), to cheer her up after the fatigues and toils of the day, he brings her a mouthful of curses and awful imprecations, and perhaps blows. Then, is he not most assuredly ten thousand times worse than any brute beast; for if any beast of prey was so fortunate as to catch more than he required ten thousand times, he would be certain to bring some home to his partner. The Malt Tax has driven the man below the standard of the brute beast which his Creator ordained him to rule and govern.

Such a state of affairs ought not to exist in this, our professedly Christian country. I have no doubt there are, daily, thousands of aching hearts, and not a few limbs, all attributable, more or less, to this iniquitous tax, tempting the man to leave his wife and family, instead of spending his evenings at home, and enjoying pure, wholesome beer at his own fireside, together with his wife and children.

Why on earth should not the wife enjoy, and be able to have her half a pint of beer as well as the husband? What happiness can there be, when one is mad from having taken too much, and the other worn out with fatigue from not having any? Such a state of things was never intended, and ought not to remain. Good, wholesome malt liquor is recommended by the faculty for the infirm and needy generally, and more particularly for mothers when nursing their infants; but very few of the labouring classes can obtain it in a pure state.

The Tax operates most cruelly in prohibiting the use of this necessary sustenance, and as the population increases, in like manner will the multitudinous evils attending it. Witness the mortality in our large cities and towns fearfully increasing, and cleverly attributed by *some* to causes *remote* from the truth, when in most cases good, wholesome, unadulterated beer would be all that was required to avert and remove the evil complained of.

Good, wholesome beer would also prevent many diseases, especially in young and weak persons. If one part is weak, another is; consequently, the digestive organs become weak, and cannot perform their proper functions; and if they do not, a host of complaints may attack the patient at any time. There are thousands of both sexes, young and old, that die annually for the want of a little wholesome ale (although, at the same time, I readily admit there are numbers who die from excess in *eating* as well as drinking), and there are thousands that never arrive at that stage which nature designed them to be, for want of it. Poor emaciated (*beings* they are not) shadows of something, for want of strength inwardly, their chests and shoulders contract, and consumption follows. In others deformity in the spine, or one shoulder, all from weakness, which a fair portion of good ale would avert.

Thousands there are of poor girls, from the age of five to fourteen, toiling all the week in our large manufacturing towns for the small sum of two or three shillings per week; and after eking out a small pittance for the Sunday, how can they afford to purchase even a small

B

quantity of the deleterious mixture? I will not attempt to disgrace my pen by writing they are paid *less* than that sum, but I greatly fear it is more than probable.

What a different race would these poor children soon become if they could only get one half-pint of good beer per day! Only one half-pint! Is it possible in our boasted free country that these poor girls should be deprived of this small quantity of necessary sustenance. Does it not, indeed, deprive them of muscle, thereby robbing them of those personal charms which nature and their Creator designed them to be proud and take care of. How seldom does one see the lovely perfection of nature's beauty among the poorer classes, especially in large towns and cities, and all for the want of a little unadulterated, wholesome beer.

Tens of thousands there are that go to bed in the cold winter's night, with shivering limbs and aching hearts, for the want of one pint of that for which they toiled in the heat of the previous summer to produce, and yet cannot even get so much as a taste without being taxed. What happiness, indeed, there would again be in store for the poor man and his

wife, sauntering round the fields on a summer's
evening, watching the progress of the beautiful
crop which is to produce for them that
necessary adjunct for the completion and perfection of a cheerful and happy fireside, and at
the same time weaning him from the alehouse
alike in summer as in winter.

There cannot possibly be any inducement
for the labouring man to take an evening's
walk, and admire with gratitude and heartfelt
thanks to a kind Providence, for the growing
crops of a bountiful harvest, unless it were
placed within his reach. Here, again, is
another serious and dreadful evil attending
this iniquitous tax. The poor and ignorant
man has not the opportunity for praising and
thanking his Maker for the bountiful gifts
bestowed upon him, so often as he ought ; he
knows he has assisted in preparing the soil,
sowing, and after cultivation ; he knows the
produce is taxed beyond his reach ; he takes
no interest therein to watch the progress of
the crop, and consequently loses many oppor-
tunities of being reminded of, and thanking
his Maker for his many and past mercies.

But what does he do may be asked; why
he goes to the alehouse and blasphemes and

takes his Maker's name in vain, for allowing such a tax to remain on his natural, and national, and only beverage. Are there not thousands of poor women whose lives are saved when in a weak state from *natural* causes with a fair allowance of wholesome beer, even in an adulterated state. Did He who sent everything for some wise purpose, and more especially that which was intended to comfort and relieve the poor in their afflicted state,—did He intend that such should be taxed? Certainly not; then most assuredly it must be awfully displeasing to Him that that article should be taxed which is most conducive to the well-being of those whom He chose to create, and whom He strictly enjoins us to love and cherish and not oppress. It is a curse upon this boastedly Christian country; it not only is the cause of all vice and crime in its most hideous forms, but it is endeavouring to thwart an All Wise Providence from the carrying on and fulfilment of His bountiful and merciful designs.

What is wine, or for whom is it intended? For shame! Can I allow my pen to say it is for the rich, and not be able to say the poor man can have his beer? Was it not always intended ever since our Saviour's appearance on earth that wine should be taken when required, to gladden man's heart, cheer his drooping spirits and refresh his weary body?

Beer is the poor man's wine. It is his right, and who dares to deny it in the face of Him who sent it as the *only* beverage he can get? Are we not all of the same flesh and blood? The Great One that made the rich man made the poor man, and looks down upon him with compassionate mercy, and sees that he is ill-treated. Therefore it is evidently obvious that it behoves us as a Christian country, without hesitation, to repeal the whole tax at once, and place the poor man's wine within his reach. The longer we defer it the greater is our sin, for every hour—and I say, every minute—adds to the crime that is alone attributable to this unlawful and abominably demoralizing tax.

"Thou shalt not muzzle the ox that treadeth out the corn." Is not this injunction sufficient to incite every living man to bestir himself, and insist upon the immediate and total repeal of the tax? The poor man is muzzled whilst he is treading out the corn, for he certainly does tread out a great deal during the operation of thrashing, either by the flail *or* machine; he does not, nor does he *wish* to eat a portion of the *corn*, but he is naturally supposed to entertain a craving desire for it in a *liquid* state when manufactured into beer, to refresh and strengthen his weary body for the toils of the following day; and if he does not, or cannot get any during the hours of *work*, it must necessarily be a great source of comfort to him, in looking forward all day until the time shall arrive in the evening to join his wife and family, by his own fireside, in the enjoyment of his right and national beverage. I will venture to guarantee that not one man in fifty, after having returned to his home and eaten his dinner, with a pint or two of good beer in the evening, will entertain the slightest wish to resort to the alehouse.

This is another convincing proof that the tax is both oppressive and unlawful. How beautifully the surpassing delight of a domestic fireside is described in the fine old song, "Home, home, sweet, sweet home; there's no place like home!" But, alas, where is it to be found? and if you find one, how far is it on to the next? and lastly, how is it to be obtained? Landed Proprietors and Members of Parliament exert yourselves, and vote for the total repeal of the tax which will put the British farmer in the position he *ought* to be; and also in a position to pay the poor man higher wages, which will enable him to pay *such* rent as shall return *sufficient* interest to the landlord for the outlay of his capital. Here is at once the two-fold advantage—the poor man in a position to rent a comfortable *house* instead of a hovel, and also in a position to procure *that* which will make it comfortable inside.

It is universally admitted that the decencies of life should be preserved, and it is proved that farm labourers live in a condition that does not accord with reasonable ideas of propriety.

Since the repeal of the corn laws the price of all sorts of corn has fallen considerably, but the tenant's obligations to his landlord are unaltered, and he is obliged to retrench, and economize in labour as in everything else, to enable him to get a livelihood ; therefore, unless some decided change is made, the farmer cannot afford to pay higher wages.

The landed proprietors, with the assistance of their agents, are generally astute enough to know what scheme best to adopt to maintain the price of the soil (one especially, namely, to lessen the number of farms by increasing the size of them, so that the demand shall be greater than the supply); but they seem to lose sight of the advantages they would derive from the abolition of the Malt tax. It is undoubtedly a landlord's question, and the majority of Members of Parliament are landed proprietors, they have the whole case in their hands, it is their duty to abolish the tax without delay, and by so doing they will benefit themselves, benefit the farmer, confer the greatest possible boon on the poor man, and increase the comforts and joys of his home a hundredfold.

A clean fireside and smiles sincere,—
Where is the heart they would not cheer?

But let me ask what inducement is there for a wife to get a clean fireside, when her husband does not care to share it with her; and if she does how heart-rending must it be when he returns from rolling in the mud like a beast from the effects of intoxication, never heeding to clean his feet, and emitting the foulest of language from his mouth, and all from the effects of this demoralizing tax.

Where after a short time will the "stout
hearts of Britain" be found? where shall we
find the jolly sailors and active recruits?
Alas, not in England! Thousands there are
that annually leave our Sister country, and we
are already following in the same wake. The
Malt tax is gradually melting down the sinews
of war!

This iniquitous tax involves the extortion
of four profits from the poor man's crop, after
he has assisted to harvest the same, before he
can moisten his lips with his own rightful and
lawful beverage. Firstly, there is the tax,
secondly, the maltster, thirdly, the brewer, and
fourthly, the publican, making in all something like 120 per cent. above the average
price of barley; and if we were to calculate
upon the unnecessary quantity drunk, caused
by the unnatural thirst created by the effects
of adulteration, it would, I have no doubt,
reach 200 per cent.

Then, again, there is another great evil
attending the tax. If tobacco is used in the
process of brewing beer, for what purpose is it
intended after the principal properties are
extracted? Why it is dried and sold to the
poor man in the shape of cheap tobacco, rob-

bing him again of the genuine article. Are there not many signs and warnings to show us that we do oppress the poor man; I say *we*, because it is entirely our own fault if we allow it to remain.

There is a cause for everything; remove that cause and the effect will cease. Let us one and all unite, join hand in hand, and remove this oppressive tax; we shall then see if we have not removed a cause for some of the awful visitations which it has pleased the Almighty to inflict upon us. If we see an injury done to another, and quietly look on without trying to avert it when it is in our power to do so, we are as much to blame as those who commit the injury complained of.

There is another very important point (connected with the poor man's welfare), showing how cruelly the tax operates against him. If he had the free use of Malt he could fatten his pig at least at one-third less cost; he could also fatten a few rabbits for the market every week. There is nothing that will fatten a rabbit so quickly as malt, and a fortnight at least will be all the time required. The poor man's wife would then be able to keep the grocer and draper in check, and with the ready

money in her hand obtain all that was necessary at one-third less cost.

Thousands of labourers there are who cannot pay at the shop but once a year, namely,
after harvest; and what a frightful bill it is—
at least one-third more than it should have
been. Extravagance creeps in and economy
walks out; and from paying only once a year
there is no inducement to economize. If, on
the other hand, the poor man were in a better
position (which he will be when the tax is
repealed), his wife would be enabled to go to
shop once a week with so much money, she
would get into a habit of paying cash for
everything, and if there were any other article
she fancied she wanted, and the cash did not
hold out, she would go home without it; but
when the bill is only paid once a year such
economizing habits are never acquired.

I think I have sufficiently explained how
cruelly this unlawful tax operates against the
poor man; I will now endeavour to show how
it oppresses the farmer. The farmer is undoubtedly the greatest sufferer. He suffers
from the oppression of the tax without, and if
he has the smallest particle of feeling he must
suffer from within, from the idea that he is

compelled to lower the price of labour in order to meet his own demands.

As regards the feeding properties of malt, there can be but one opinion, namely, that there cannot be found anywhere on the face of the earth any sort of food that will fatten cattle and sheep so quickly, and impart that sweet and agreeable flavour to the flesh, as malt.

To make farming profitable, it ought strictly to be (as near as possible) a self-supporting establishment ; therefore the farmer ought to be allowed to grow, or to manu-facture that which he requires for his stock, without being unlawfully taxed. If it were not for this iniquitous tax, the produce of our farms would supply their own wants.

Malt would supersede oil-cake and all foreign feeding stuffs. Every farmer is cog-nizant of the fact that malt dust is a valuable food for cattle and sheep, calves and pigs ; in fact, every living animal is improved in appearance by a small quantity. You cannot possibly put it in the wrong place. It is an excellent manure for any crop, especially a root crop ; a good, wholesome, and forcing food for cattle and sheep to eat with that crop ; a cheap and useful article, with other corn, for fattening pigs, and also to preserve the bacon in after having been cured ; and invaluable to all sorts of cattle and poultry, young or old, when the bowels are inclined to be relaxed.

If the dust is of so much importance, malt must be most assuredly still more so. I do not consider that malt would be a wholesome article of food if given in large quantities, nor alone; it should, in my opinion, be mixed with offal of some sort, or inferior corn or meal. Malt dust is of a constipating nature, and it must necessarily follow that malt is still more so ; therefore it should be used with caution at first.

That extraordinary results are likely to be achieved from feeding on malt, no practical agriculturist can deny. The flavour of the flesh must be far superior from cattle or sheep fattened with sugar, than from those fattened on either starch or oil ; for there is sugar in malt, starch in the meal of all corn, and oil in oil-cake, part of which is extracted from the seeds of some of the most noxious weeds that grow on the face of the earth.

Since the British farmer has been robbed

of protection, the only chance he has is to breed, rear, and fatten stock, to supply meat for the community; then, surely, he ought to be allowed to avail himself of that which is the most nutritious of all feeding stuffs.

Tens of thousands of pounds there are annually paid away from this country for foreign feeding stuffs, namely, for nearly 200,000 tons of oil-cake, nearly $1\frac{1}{2}$ millions of qrs. of linseed, part of which is converted into English cake, and about 3,000,000 qrs. of Indian corn, besides large quantities of lentils, locust beans, and a host of other foreign productions.

Those who are opposed to the abolition of the tax have not, nor can have, the slightest foundation to argue upon. They may say we want the duty off tea, sugar, life, fire, and other insurance offices. The argument does not apply; firstly, tea and sugar are both cheaper at the present time than beer will be when the Malt Tax is repealed; one lb. of tea will last a family of four or five persons one month with careful management, which would be four shillings; and one quart only of best beer (with the abolition of the tax) per day will be threepence, which will be seven shillings for the month, and if the twelvemonth's consumption of tea were bought in a chest at once it may be procured at three shillings and sixpence per lb., which would then be only half the price of the month's consumption of beer.

Secondly, as regards insurance offices, &c. If the tax is abolished labour will be cheaper, consequently the expenses of the establishment must diminish in like proportion. I consider it needless to argue at any great length on the sugar duty, suffice it to say, that that article will (in the event of the repeal of the tax) work itself aright, and eventually be much lower in price.

There are no doubt thousands of tons of sugar used in the process of brewing, which will not be required when every man is allowed to brew his own beer, and that will make a greater difference than all the duty on that article.

It is now something like twenty years since that the measure for "free imports" was carried, and yet the Malt duty (a disgrace to the principles of free trade) still remains, and will continue to exist as an impediment to the farming interest until it is abolished. Why should agriculture be thus fettered as it were in chains of restriction, when it is the first and most honourable of all occupations, as borne out by the fact of Adam having been called forth to till the soil previous to any other employment?

It must be obvious to every one, that to tax the raw material is decidedly wrong, and contrary to the dictates of reason and principle; and at the same time opening a field of the widest possible margin for adulteration.

Is it not indeed thwarting the designs of Him who called man forth to till the land, and to live by the sweat of his brow? Most assuredly we can, if we chose, find ample proof to convince us that it is decidedly unconstitutional and unlawful.

Look at the glaring fact of the sole object of this fictitious free trade, to advance and encourage the prosperity of the manufacturing districts at the ruinous expense of the farmer. Have we not had sufficient warning? Look at the distress which has already existed, and may still exist, among the starving thousands.

Did they on the eve of the fictitious free trade ever dream of a cotton famine? Certainly not. Then cannot the All Wise Providence that sent it, also send a famine in corn? Look at the fearful war raging in America, and the whole Continent ready to burst into flames. The farmer has been grievously and sorely oppressed, and the time of retribution will most assuredly come.

How many there are that argue on the impropriety of a host of taxes, comparing them with the Malt tax, insinuating that it is only another name for beer. Why do they not talk of taxing the young foal, that is to grow up to draw the vehicle they intend to hire and pay taxes for, or the sapling oak, ash, or elm, which is intended a hundred years hence to build the same.

Can it be fair and just to allow the foreigner to make use of our Malt free of duty, fatten his cattle and sheep, and send them to us *without* duty, while we ourselves are *deprived* of that opportunity? If so, let it remain ; if not, then the dictates of principle plainly tell us we should at once repeal this unlawful tax.

There are some who attempt to argue on the unfairness of the assessed taxes, as being inquisitorial and vexatious. The class to whom those taxes apply can well afford to pay. The

c

horse and dog are not taxed until arrived at maturity and fit for use, nor should malt be taxed until matured in the shape of beer and fit to drink.

Hundreds of thousands of acres there are lying waste in the United Kingdom that could profitably be made available for the growth of barleys, and other crops would necessarily follow, were it not for the injurious operation of the tax. With other crops in the course of rotation, the root crop would be greatly increased, which would increase the quantity of meat, and consequently diminish the price. This clearly shows again, how cruelly the tax operates on the poor man; deprived of pure beer, and deprived even of impure meat, for tens of thousands of lbs. of impure meat are sold at a price that the poor man cannot possibly reach.

Are we then in a professedly Christian country supposed to be doing our duty to the poor? No, far indeed from it. The question may be asked how it is to be done? Why by abolishing the unlawful tax which will enable the poor man to obtain his pure beer, pure tobacco, and also enable him to procure a bit of pure meat at least once in the week.

Why should the poor man be treated like a beast, and the farmer bound in chains whilst the foreigner is free? Such a state of affairs ought not to exist ; it is a disgrace to the country and its population. We ought to demand the repeal of the tax as a right, and not as a favour. The farmers of England stand alone as regards taxation, (foreign producers using their produce without paying duty,) while they themselves have to pay a duty of 75 per cent. The Malt tax is a robbery of the farmer and poor man, and we have no one to blame but ourselves, if we do not obtain a faithful promise at the next election for its total repeal.

But I see no reason for waiting until that period shall arrive; all that is required is, for those who are for the total repeal to demand it as an Englishman's right. Who dares to deny him? Right will always overcome might, if unity is applied for the accomplishment of the object. Those who are against the repeal of the tax may just as well remain silent and cheerfully submit, for it must come sooner or later, as a just and lawful decision of our honourable Members, whose sacred duty it is to devise those means best adapted for raising *such* taxes as shall bear equally on *all* classes without favour or affection, with profound discretion and totally *exempt* from the slightest tint of oppression.

He that knowingly oppresseth the poor woe be unto him. Millions of peasants there are *poor* we know, and are there not thousands of poor farmers, who cannot afford to supply themselves with a sufficient quantity of their indigenous beverage (namely, malt liquor), meat, tea, sugar, cheese, butter, or genuine tobacco, and all from the cause of this abominable tax.

I have no doubt there are many who will be curious enough to express a wish for an explanation, in what manner the Malt tax can possibly interfere with all these common necessaries. I have already stated how it affects the price of sugar, and partly so on meat and tobacco ; I will now endeavour to show how it affects each article separately and connectively.

Firstly, beer, owing to the tax, calculating on a series of adulteration, is 150 per cent. dearer than it ought to be ; but with the abolition of the tax, and taking into consideration the increased consumption which must necessarily follow, it will naturally enhance the price of barley, which will then reduce it to 100 per cent., namely, that on the immediate repeal of the tax best beer will fall in price to something like 8d. per gallon, but from the increased demand will soon advance to one shilling per gallon, at which price it can be manufactured with barley ranging in price from 50s. to 60s. per quarter, which will be at the price that wheat ought to be, and it cannot be grown profitably much under that price. The British farmer would then occupy his rightful position, which would enable him to make the poor man's home comfortable. Would it not indeed be glorious days for the farmer and his servants? pouring forth everlasting praises and acclamations of joy to Him who delights in the happiness of His people.

If the British farmer is robbed of his price for wheat, it is common justice to him to be allowed to make up that deficiency on some other crop whenever an opportunity occurs. The fair average price of wheat for all parties was formerly considered and calculated to be about 60s. per quarter, and barley at 30s. per quarter; then if wheat is to be brought down to the price of barley, is it not fair and just that that article shall be allowed to advance and approximate the price at which wheat was considered to be remunerative to the grower?

Secondly, with regard to meat of all sorts, that article would fall in price one penny at least, if not twopence, per lb., because not only will that article (namely, Malt) be manufactured at home, where it is used, saving unnecessary cartage, and containing the most nutritious properties of all feeding stuffs, but it will also in a great measure avert the multitudinous diseases with which our young stock *particularly* are liable to be afflicted in this variable climate.

With regard to its fat and flesh making capabilities there cannot be but one opinion, namely, that it supersedes every other sort of feeding stuff.

The Chancellor of the Exchequer argues that he is not convinced of the favourable results supposed to accrue from Malt feeding; he knows full well that owing to the heavy duty the farmer has not had the opportunity to experimentalize on the valuable feeding properties of Malt to any extent, and on this basis alone he argues. But with all due deference to him he must not suppose the

British farmer, in these enlightened days
(whatever he may have been a century ago),
is so ignorant, and devoid of all knowledge of
chemistry, that he cannot test and ascertain
the valuable properties of *one* feeding stuff
over another in a few minutes, instead of
waiting for a period of four or five months,
until his cattle or sheep are fed, fattened, sold
and money told.

The flesh of all malt-fed cattle and sheep
would be far superior, and much sweeter in
flavour, than those fattened on oilcake adulterated with sand (which can be bought at
10s. per ton, and is sold at £10 per ton) and
foreign seeds of weeds of the most noxious
kind.

Every practical farmer and grazier is cog-
nizant of the fact, that hitherto there is no
flesh equal in point of flavour and sweetness
to that which is fed on grass, or good hay and
turnips; and whilst Malt would impart an
additional flavour and sweetness, it would also
prepare cattle and sheep for the market in half
the time.

Thirdly, with regard to sugar, that article is
very easily explained in a few words. Owing
to the high price of Malt the field is wide, and

the temptation great, for adulteration. As before stated, there are no doubt thousands of tons of sugar used in the process of brewing. If the tax is abolished there will be none required for that purpose, there will not be so much competition in the sugar market, and consequently the price must be lower; I shall also presently point out another reason why the abolition of the tax will lower the price of sugar.

What a boon for the public! and what a necessary adjunct to the morning and evening meals of tens of thousands of starving children. Many thousands there are who would be perfectly satisfied, and thrive and do well on oat-meal porridge, when made palatable with a sufficient quantity of sugar, which would not exceed more than twopence or threepence per lb.

And now, fourthly, how will it affect the tea market? Why all the labouring classes at noon invariably make a grand tea meal, and that being the only beverage within their reach they generally make it pretty good, for they find that a cup of good tea is very refreshing for a short time, but it does not last for many hours. Now good wholesome beer would be equally refreshing, and give additional strength for the remainder of the day. With the repeal of the Malt duty they will be enabled to obtain that luxury, and consequently they will dispense with the mid-day tea meal, and gladly avail themselves of the opportunity.

Assuming that the poorer classes represent more that half of the entire population, and that they do as a body consume more than half the tea imported, and presuming that they would take half the quantity they did before, it must necessarily lessen the consumption one-fourth, more or less, and consequently lower prices must follow. With this arrangement there will be less sugar *again* required, which will still lower the price of that article. And now, my dearly beloved teetotallers, what say you to the Malt tax? Is it not apparent to you all, if the tax were abolished, that it would be conferring upon you one of the *greatest* blessings on earth, namely, *cheap* tea and sugar.

Fifthly, there will not be so much, if any tobacco required in the process of brewing. Thousands of lbs. there are, I have no doubt, as before stated, used in the manufacturing of beer; some, perhaps, dried and sold again, but the *bulk*, I suspect, would be consumed in the furnace to avoid detection. Is not this a gross piece of injustice and fraud towards the exchequer? However, with the total repeal of the tax, there will be no more tobacco required for brewing purposes; consequently the poor man will then be able to get genuine tobacco, as well as the gentleman his genuine cigar, and at one-third, if not half, the price he has been hitherto obliged to pay.

Sixthly, there is another cause why the tax oppresses the poor man. Owing to the operation of the tax he cannot procure a sufficient quantity of cheese and butter; the poorer classes, not being able to obtain beer, devour so much extra milk per day with their meagre tea meal, which must necessarily diminish the production of the above-named articles; and anyone who thinks fit to dispute the fact, let them take notice at the various railway stations and daily witness the huge tin vessels filled with milk, and consigned to our large cities and towns for the teeming population.

I consider there are 3,000,000 pints of milk, more or less, consumed daily, to render the tea palatable for the unnecessary tea meal, which is 375,000 gallons. Now 3 gallons of milk will make one lb. of cheese, and that quantity amounts to 125,000 lbs. of cheese daily, and 45,525,000 annually, which, at 6d. per lb., will realize the sum of £1,140,625. Now with regard to butter, if such a description of cheese is only worth 6d. per lb., we infer there must be a great quantity of butter also made from this quantity of milk; hence the cause of the dearness of these articles of domestic comfort, and which will and must continue to increase so long as this unjust tax is allowed to remain.

Seventhly, there is a cause why the large consumption of milk increases the price of pork. If the 375,000 gallons of milk were converted into cheese (besides the butter), there must necessarily be daily as many as 300,000 gallons of whey, more or less; now that quantity will feed 100,000 small pigs, and they would gain in weight 5 lbs. per head per week, which will be 500,000 lbs. of pork per week, and 26,000,000 lbs. per annum, and, at 6d. per lb., will be £650,000. Here again is a great waste of the common necessaries of domestic comfort, and attributable alone to the unjustness of the tax.

It must be apparent to every one who knows any thing of country life, and acquainted with the animal and vegetable kingdom, that the sweetest food for cattle will produce the sweetest flesh and finest flavoured. Will not venison and Welsh mountain mutton bear ample testimony to the fact? for we know that deer and wild sheep are continually nipping the sweetest of vegetation, and more especially the sweet wild thyme and buds from the shoots of trees, all of which contain a deal of sugar. Grain ground into meal is simply starch and nothing more; now when converted into malt it is sugar in the highest perfection, and hence the reason that malt will make sweeter and finer flavoured flesh than any other feeding stuff. But it must not be given in large quantities with mangold wurtzel; it is adding sugar to honey, and cattle will not thrive fast on sugar alone. The right and proper sorts of roots to feed, in conjunction with malt, would be swedes, turnips, potatoes, &c., and corn meal, or such articles of food that contains starch ; but the greatest advantage to be derived from malt feeding would be found in giving it to sheep while they are consuming the turnips on the soil.

Eighthly and lastly, with the free use of malt the health of animals would be greatly improved, a multitude of diseases would be averted, and consequently there would be more pure, and less impure, meat sent to market, which must necessarily diminish the mortality in our large cities and towns. Every medical man must be aware of the fact that impure meat is unwholesome, and that a continual use of it must naturally impair the human constitution, and lay a foundation for innumerable diseases. In conclusion, I may add the Malt tax is so abominably iniquitous and unjust, that there is scarcely any article of consumption that will not be benefitted by its total repeal.

Every one knows that barley is taxed higher than any other article of produce in the country, but why relieve it ? is the question. Would beer be cheaper ? Would the land profit by its total repeal ? and a host of other questions are asked.

Why it is obvious to every one, from what I have stated, that the demand for barley will be boundless, that its price will nearly double and that beer will be reduced to half its present price : the following articles of consumption must also be cheaper, meat of all sorts, poultry, game, and fish, cheese, butter, sugar, tea, tobacco, snuff, vinegar, &c., &c.

Some may raise the question how on earth can it affect the price of vinegar? Why tens of thousands of poor souls there are, who buy their half a pint of vinegar at a time, more or less, for salad in the summer, and greens or cabbage in the winter, to impart a sort of zest or relish to their meagre food.

Now, in the first place, with plenty of good wholesome beer, they will not require it, and secondly, every one knows that vinegar and beer do not relish together.

With regard to land, such soils as are calculated, and best adapted for the growth of barley, will be eagerly sought after, owing to the easy manner in which they are cultivated; consequently, land will be benefitted by the repeal of the tax.

Now, the next all-important question is— Can the Chancellor of the Exchequer afford to lose the tax? I say yes. I do not say where he is to retrench, for it does not devolve upon me to dictate to the Chancellor of the Exchequer where he can, and when he cannot curtail the expenses of the country, nor is it in accordance with my object.

If he says, No, I cannot afford to lose the tax, I will endeavour to point out how the difficulty is to be surmounted. That the raw material should be taxed every one knows is unfair and unjust, then if the Chancellor of the Exchequer wishes to find a substitute, let him tax that beer which is sold and no other, at the same rate as it is taxed now at the present time, namely, one penny per quart.

Now we will suppose there would be 2,400,000 quarts per day sold, including exports, that quantity would bring in a revenue of £3,650,000, or twopence per quart may be levied on half that quantity, which amounts to the same sum, or a tax of threepence per quart may be placed on a still smaller quantity, and the consumer would even then get it as cheap as at the present time; there will be no excuse then for the poor man's visit to the alehouse, especially if he finds he has to pay double the sum for which he can produce the liquor at home.

The consumption at home, with the exports, would increase to an immense extent with the abolition of the tax, as will be seen by the statistics below.

In 1722, when there was no duty, more malt was consumed in England by six millions

.of people than was consumed by twelve
millions in 1822 when the duty was 3s. 7½d. a
bushel, and not until the duty fell to 2s. 7d.
per bushel in 1832 did the English people
drink so much beer, as they did with not half
the population one hundred and ten years
previously.

There is also another substitute for the
malt tax which I mentioned to Capt. Vernon,
of Ardington, Wantage, and M.P. for the
county of Berks, only a fortnight before he
died, namely, that a penny stamp be stamped
on all third-class railway tickets. The poor
man will not object if he knows he is to have
his quart of good beer for threepence.

Other classes, I believe, are taxed 5 per
cent., but even then there is nothing so very
alarming to stamp those tickets also with the
penny stamp. The traveller would not then
be taxed so high as he was in the old posting
days; however, the poor man, or labouring
class, or say third-class passengers, will not
object to pay an extra penny for a journey,
when they know on their arrival at their
destination they will be able to obtain a quart
of good wholesome ale for threepence, and
that alone I consider would be sufficient to fill

up the gap caused by the abolition of the malt tax.

Teetotallers, perhaps, will not agree to this arrangement, but let them remember, as I have before stated, it is to their advantage also; for whilst they would be assisting in conferring an act of charity on others, they would be benefitting themselves on every article of consumption. Then to conclude and sum up, if third-class passengers come forward and are willing to pay the penny stamp, in order to obtain their national and only beverage, in a pure and wholesome state, who dares to deny them? Let, then, every man, woman, and child, that can write and affix a signature, send a petition immediately to the Chancellor of the Exchequer, praying for a total repeal of this cruel and oppressive tax.

PRINTED AT THE "CHRONICLE" OFFICE, KINGSTON BUILDINGS, BATH.

www.ingramcontent.com/pod-product-compliance
Lightning Source LLC
Chambersburg PA
CBHW031815090426
42739CB00008B/1282